WATER POWER
Richard and Louise Spilsbury

WAYLAND

First published in 2007
by Wayland

Copyright © Wayland 2007

Wayland
338 Euston Road
London NW1 3BH

Wayland Australia
Level 17/207 Kent Street
Sydney NSW 2000

Series Editor: Jennifer Schofield
Editor: Susie Brooks
Consultant: Rob Bowden
Designer: Jane Hawkins
Cover design: Paul Cherrill
Picture Research: Diana Morris
Artwork: Ian Thompson
Indexer: Sue Lightfoot

Picture Acknowledgments:
Sue Anderson/Ecoscene: 24. Aquatera.co.uk: 45. Martin Bond/SPL: 15.
Anthony Cooper/Ecoscene: 7. Michel Coupard/StillPictures: 18.
Joel Creed/Ecoscene: 1, Jerzy Dabrowski/epa/Corbis: front cover.
EASI Images: 4, 11, 39. ESA: 27. Alexandra Elliot Jones/Ecoscene: 30.
Hank Morgan/SPL: 36. © Ocean Power Delivery: 17. © Ocean Power
Technologies Ltd : 42. Christine Osborne/Ecoscene: 22. Robert Slade/
PhotographersDirect: 35. Stuckmann/Still Pictures: 33. Bjorn Svensson/
Ecoscene: 20. Ami Vitale/GettyImages: 28.

Every attempt has been made to clear copyright. Should there be any
inadvertent omission please apply to the publisher for rectification.

CIP data
Spilsbury, Richard, 1963
Water power. - (Energy debate)
1. Water-power - Juvenile literature
I. Title II Spilsbury, Louise
333.9'14

ISBN 978 07502 5021 4

Printed in China

Wayland is a division of Hachette Children's Books

Note:

Contents

CHAPTER 1 Water power and the energy debate

The energy that people use to make electricity comes from different sources. Worldwide, some energy sources, such as oil, are running out – but others, such as moving water and sunlight, are plentiful. People are debating which sources of energy they should use now and into the future.

Energy sources

There are two broad categories of energy sources. Non-renewables are sources that cannot be replaced once they are used up. These include fossil fuels, such as coal and natural gas, and nuclear fuels. Fossil fuels are the remains of ancient plants and animals that died millions of years ago, and nuclear fuels are harnessed from the energy found in the atoms of metals such as uranium. Most of the world's power comes from non-renewables, but they are in limited supply.

Renewable energy sources will not run out. These include solar energy (light and heat from the Sun's rays) and geothermal energy (heat from deep inside Earth). Renewable fuel called biogas is made from rotting plant and animal waste. Water power and wind power are also generated using renewable energy found in moving water and air.

▽ Smog, as seen here in busy Beijing, China, is caused by polluting gases that react with sunlight.

Converting energy

When energy is used, it does not disappear but simply changes form. This principle is called the conservation of energy. Most electricity is made using generators. These are machines that turn movement, or kinetic, energy into electrical energy. In water and wind power systems, rushing water and wind provide kinetic energy directly, by pushing against turbine blades that twist and make generators work. Fuels create kinetic energy in a more indirect way. First of all, the fuels react to change their stored energy into heat energy. Many fuels burn, or react with oxygen in air, and the heat produced is used to boil water, creating high-pressure steam. The moving water molecules in steam provide kinetic energy.

Permanent pollution

Non-renewable resources are not only limited in supply; they also cause a major problem – pollution. When fossil fuels burn, they release waste gases. Some of these gases, such as sulphur dioxide, cause air pollution, affecting breathing and producing damaging acid rain. Others, including carbon dioxide and methane, build up in the atmosphere, trapping the Sun's heat near Earth's surface. This is called the greenhouse effect. It is making Earth's climate warmer and affecting weather around the globe. There are other problems too, such as damage to the environment by mining and drilling for non-renewable fuels.

THE ARGUMENT: Renewables are better than non-renewables

For:
- Renewable resources are free and in endless supply.
- Fuel is not burned so there is minimal air pollution.
- People do not have to dig or drill into the ground for these resources.
- There are no waste-disposal problems as there are, for example, for used nuclear fuel.

Against:
- New technology can make non-renewables cleaner, for example filters on power station chimneys.
- Power from renewable energy is often more expensive than from non-renewables.
- Some non-renewables, such as coal, are not yet in dangerously short supply.

Looming energy crisis

Many people believe that the world is on the verge of an energy crisis. Demand for power from existing sources will soon be greater than the amount produced. A major reason for this is the rapidly growing population.

There are about three times more people on Earth now than there were in 1950. More and more people rely increasingly on electrical appliances, from kettles to computers. Based on current rates of use, scientists predict that some non-renewables, such as oil, will run out in less than 50 years. As fuel supplies dwindle, so they will cost more to buy. This energy crisis, and the growing evidence for climate change, has caused many people to look more closely at renewable energy for their power needs.

" Not only will atomic power be released, but some day we will harness the rise and fall of the tides and imprison the rays of the Sun. **"**

Thomas A. Edison, US inventor (1847–1931), 22 August 1921

Renewables in the mix

The range of energy sources any region uses for power is called its energy mix. Most regions generate some electricity using non-renewables and some using renewables. The mix varies at different scales, from continent to country and from city to individual. For example, overall the USA gets 10 per cent of its electricity from water power. However, this percentage varies by state, owing mostly to local geography. The figure for Washington, which has lots of rivers moving down its mountains, is 80 per cent – but that for Florida, which is very flat with slow rivers, is barely 5 per cent.

Another reason why a region may use renewable energy sources is isolation. About a third of the global population has no access to electricity made in large power stations. One of the only ways these communities, such as those on the slopes of the Himalayas in Nepal, can get electricity is by using small-scale water power schemes.

Using water to do our work

Water-powered machines are not new. In Ancient Greece, around 4,000 years ago, people used wheels turned by falling water to grind wheat into flour. Water-powered bellows blew air into furnaces in China at around the same time, keeping fires burning hot enough to melt metals. Other water-powered machines of the past included pumps, saws and clocks. In countries such as the USA and the UK, water wheels ran most machines up to the early 19th century. Then steam power took over, because coal to burn in steam engines became cheaper and more widely available after canals and railways were built. The first use of moving water to generate electricity dates back to the 1880s, when generators were first fitted to water wheels. The technology spread and improved in many regions. In the late 20th century, people also learned how to generate power using ocean waves and tides.

▽ This waterwheel in Bayeux, France, provided water power for a mill. Flowing water pushed the blades, rotating a shaft which, via a series of gears, turned a millstone to grind wheat.

CHAPTER 2 How water power works

Water power relies on two things: technology to convert the force of moving water into electricity, and a plentiful source of moving water. This water can come from rivers and reservoirs, or from the oceans.

The water turbine

In most water power installations, moving water operates a turbine. A water turbine works rather like a windmill. It converts the movement of water (rather than air) into turning kinetic energy. A given volume of water is heavier than the same volume of air: it is hundreds of times denser. So water pushes against a turbine with greater force than wind does, turning the blades at a greater speed.

A turbine has a central shaft with several blades arranged around it. Depending on the turbine design, the blades can be set parallel to the shaft,

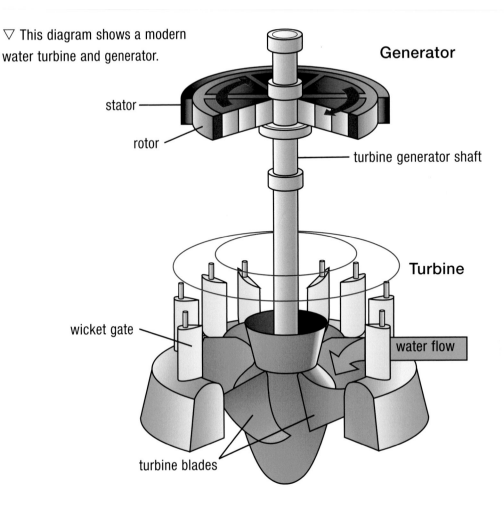

▽ This diagram shows a modern water turbine and generator.

Generator

stator

rotor

turbine generator shaft

Turbine

wicket gate

water flow

turbine blades

like a paddle wheel, or at right angles to the shaft, like a propeller on a boat. Each blade is curved to make water swirl across and against it. This makes the blades twist the shaft as much as possible with each bit of force applied by the water. Water is often channelled first into a pipe called a penstock. This directs the water straight at the blades, sometimes through angled gates. It also narrows over its length to increase the force of water hitting the blades.

> **"** Water power was the first inorganic force which man learnt to use instead of his own labour or that of domestic animals. **"**
>
> Hermann von Helmholtz, German physicist, 1821–1894

Generating electricity

The shaft is attached to a generator that produces electricity. As the shaft rotates, it turns the rotor. This is a series of very long copper wires wound into separate coils. The rotor moves inside a circular stator. The stator is made of strong magnets. When each coil passes a magnet, the magnet makes tiny particles called electrons flow inside the coil. This flow of electrons is electricity.

Electrical power is usually given in watts (W). This is a measure of both the speed of flow of electricity, and the force with which it moves through the wires. Turbine power is compared in thousands of watts (kilowatts or KW), millions of watts (megawatts or MW) or even thousands of millions of watts (gigawatts or GW).

Distributing power

Once electricity is produced, it moves through cables connected to the generator to where it is needed. Sometimes it is used near to where the turbine is situated. However, power is often needed to run machines a long way away, so turbines are usually connected to transformers. These machines increase the push of electricity so it can be transmitted at the same speed through cables stretching over long distances.

The network of continuous cables and wires that distribute electricity from water power and other energy sources is called the electrical grid. Often the grid's cabling is supported on pylons. Most homes, schools, offices, factories, streetlights and other parts of settlements are connected to the grid.

Source of water

All of the water that is used to generate electricity is part of the water cycle. This is the continuous recycling of Earth's water, driven by the enormous amounts of energy in the Sun's rays. The Sun warms water on land, for example in lakes, reservoirs and puddles, and at the surface of the oceans. Some of this water evaporates, meaning it changes from liquid to gas (vapour). The water vapour rises into the atmosphere, cools and condenses into tiny water droplets that form clouds. Droplets bump into and join with each other, forming larger drops that eventually fall to Earth as raindrops, hailstones and snow.

> **The cycle of life is intricately tied up with the cycle of water.**
>
> Jacques Cousteau, French underwater explorer and inventor

On the ground, some fallen water accumulates as ice in the coldest places, or soaks into the Earth. However, on anything but the flattest land, most water runs off the surface into gulleys and streams. Streams may carry water into lakes or run into each other, forming rivers. The area of land from which water runs off into a river is called its catchment area. Rivers may merge, forming larger rivers as they flow along. Many rivers flow towards estuaries where they meet oceans.

Head and flow rate

Water turbines generate more power the faster they spin. The energy in moving water hitting a turbine's blades depends on both its speed and the volume flowing. Water moves faster naturally when it meets a slope, because the force of gravity pulls its mass downwards. The steeper the slope, or greater the gradient, the faster water falls.

The difference in height between water level at the start and end of a slope is called the head of water. Flow rate is the volume of water passing a certain point within a particular period. The greatest water energy is a product of high flow rate and high head, and the smallest combines low flow rate and low head. However, the same power can be made from high head/low flow and low head/high flow situations.

River power

Power created using water turbines in fresh water is often called hydropower. Some hydropower projects use the energy in rivers where water

naturally changes level. These are called run-of-river projects. Some run-of-river situations have low head and high flow – for example where large rivers drop over small, wide waterfalls, such as Idaho Falls, USA. Others have high head and low flow, for example where small rivers drop fast down steep slopes. Run-of-river

△ The Iguazu falls, in Brazil, is probably the most powerful waterfall on Earth. It combines a head of 90 metres and an average flow rate equivalent to emptying an Olympic-sized swimming pool every 2.5 seconds!

turbines are placed directly in the path of rivers, or in river water diverted via a channel into a penstock.

Dams and reservoirs

Not all rivers naturally provide the right combination of head and flow rate to produce a lot of hydropower. Even if they do, power plants may be impractical to develop – for example, turbines might be difficult to build under a waterfall. Most hydropower comes from turbines in dams.

Dams are tall, very thick walls made to trap river water in deep reservoirs. Reservoirs can have many purposes, such as supplying water for homes or farms, but they also store potential energy. This energy becomes available once sluice gates in the dam are opened. Then, reservoir water rushes through a downward-pointing

penstock past turbines built into the thick dam walls. The potential energy changes first into kinetic energy and is then converted into electrical energy.

Deep water

The largest reservoirs stretch over hundreds of square kilometres and reach depths of 100 metres. Water pressure in the reservoir increases with water depth. At the reservoir surface, pressure is lowest because gravity pulls down only topmost water molecules – but deeper down, the force acts on a much larger mass of water. The sluice gate is positioned at the right depth on the dam to ensure optimum flow rate past the turbines. The difference in height between the top of the penstock, at the sluice gate, and the bottom ensures a large head of water.

▽ Cross-section of a hydropower plant.

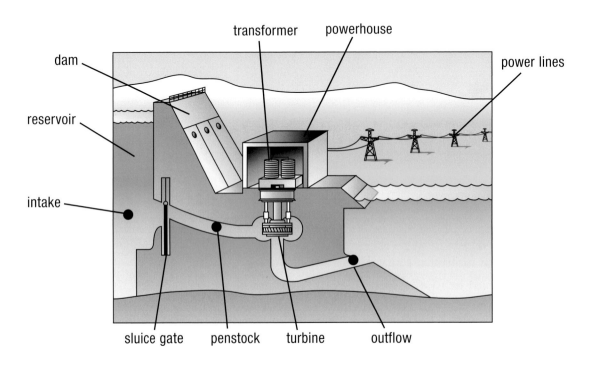

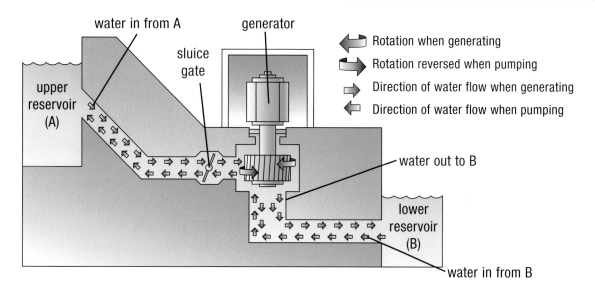

water in from A

generator

sluice
gate

Rotation when generating

Rotation reversed when pumping

Direction of water flow when generating

Direction of water flow when pumping

upper
reservoir
(A)

water out to B

lower
reservoir
(B)

water in from B

Reusing water

In many dam hydropower situations,
the water that has passed the turbines
flows into a river. Its energy is
reduced, so it no longer has any
potential for hydropower – but more
water flows into the reservoir to take
its place. In some cases, two reservoirs
are built – one at a higher level than
the other. Water stored in the upper
reservoir is released into the lower one
to operate turbines when electricity is
needed. When electricity demand is
lower, the turbines can also be used
as electric motors to operate pumps.
These transfer water back into the
upper reservoir once more. This type
of system is called pumped storage
hydropower.

Controlling power output

Rivers vary in flow rate throughout
the year owing to seasonal changes
in precipitation and temperature.

△ The pumped storage hydropower system.

For example, in a cold winter there
might be a lot of snow, but some snow
may stay frozen on the ground rather
than run off land into rivers. Rivers
may even freeze over. Lower rainfall
and higher evaporation in summer
also reduce river flow. Thus, amounts
of run-of-river hydropower may
fluctuate. All dam and reservoir
systems allow some control of
hydropower output regardless of river
flow rate, because the sluice gates are
opened only when electricity is in
demand. However, even large-capacity
river-fed reservoirs may fall in level
at some times of year. Pumped storage
systems rely less on natural river flow
because some of the water that has
passed the turbines is moved back to
the top reservoir. At the top reservoir,
it regains its potential energy for
power generation.

> **"** Roll along, Columbia, you can ramble to the sea, but river, while you're rambling, you can do some work for me. **"**
>
> Woody Guthrie, 1940s singer/songwriter, USA

History of hydropower

The history of hydropower began in 1870, when a light in the gallery of Cragside country house in northern England flickered on. It was powered by water pumped from the house's private lake past a simple generator.

The first hydropower plant, installed in Wisconsin, USA in 1882, made enough power to run 250 lights. By 1889, there were 200 small hydropower plants in the USA. Over the next 50 years hydropower grew in output. By 1940, 40 per cent of all US electricity was generated by water power – partly because turbines became more efficient and partly because bigger dams were built. This was a result of advances in engineering and also in the use of materials such as concrete, creating stronger structures to hold back larger volumes of water. But after World War II (1939–44), most new power systems were developed for fossil and nuclear fuels, and water power became a smaller part of the energy mix again.

CASE STUDY:
Eighth wonder of the world

The Grand Coulee dam on the Columbia river in Washington state, USA, was described as the eighth wonder of the world when it was completed in 1941. It contains enough concrete to build a road right across the USA. The dam was originally designed in the 1920s to provide irrigation water for farms – but World War II changed its purpose. Turbines and generators were fitted to Grand Coulee because large amounts of electricity were suddenly needed for defence industries in the north-western USA. The dam became the nation's main powerhouse for vital aluminium-producing plants, aircraft factories and shipyards on the Pacific coast. It still produces the most power of any single hydroelectric dam in the USA.

Turbine styles

There are two basic turbines used to produce water power, both designed before the first hydropower was generated. The Francis, developed in 1849, is most commonly used today. This turbine works when it is fully submerged underwater. Water moves through gaps between the curved blades out of its centre, creating a force that spins the turbine. This turbine is best suited to low head sites with a large flow rate.

The Pelton turbine was developed in the 1870s to operate mine machines that processed gold after the Gold Rush in the USA – a period when many people flocked to California to seek their fortune from mining gold. This turbine is not fully submerged. It spins fast when jets of high-pressure water hit the edge of cup-shaped blades. The Pelton is commonly used in high head, lower volume situations, such as small, fast-moving mountain streams. A later development of the Francis – the Kaplan of 1913 – looks like a ship propeller and runs best when the head of water is very low but there is a large flow rate.

▽ The distinctive double cups of the Pelton turbine were developed to convert the power of a small water jet into rotation energy.

Making waves

The world's coasts are shaped by the enormous power of waves rolling from the oceans. Waves are ultimately created by the Sun's energy. Heat from the Sun warms some air masses more than others. Warm air masses, which are less dense and lighter than cooler air masses, rise into the atmosphere, leaving behind areas of low pressure. Cooler air masses sink, pressing on the air close to Earth's surface and creating high-pressure areas. Winds blow from high- to low-pressure areas. Waves are generated by winds as they blow across the surface of oceans.

Wave energy around the world

People can use wave energy to produce power. Wave energy varies around our planet – it depends largely on the location relative to the hottest regions (near the Equator) and the cold polar masses. The greatest wave energy is generally found in areas between latitudes 40–60° in both the northern and the southern hemispheres. These include western Scotland, northern Canada and southern Africa. Such places not only have strong winds that give energy to the ocean water, creating large waves, but the winds also blow over long distances of open ocean, so they do not lose energy by passing islands and other obstructions before they reach coastlines.

Wave energy is concentrated nearest the water surface, closest to winds, and drops virtually to zero by 50 metres depth. Wave size increases in height towards coasts, because the water is forced to pile up high by the shallowing sea floor.

All at sea

Some wave power systems use the rise and fall of ocean waves. For example, the Pelamis is a hinged row of floats the length of four train carriages, which is loosely moored to the ocean floor. It swings head-on to face approaching waves. When a wave moves the first float relative to the next, it pumps oil through tubes past a mini-turbine that spins a generator. This is repeated as the wave passes each float. Electricity generated by each float moves from the Pelamis through a submerged cable to the coast. The system is designed to float just beneath the ocean surface and to be strong enough not to break in the very high waves that form in storms.

On the rocks

Other wave power systems rely on the force of waves hitting the coastline. An example is the Limpet, built on the Scottish island of Islay. This is attached to a natural rock gulley that concentrates waves towards it. As a wave hits the Limpet, a large volume of seawater, full of powerful kinetic energy, pours into a hollow chamber. The shape of the chamber is rather like an inverted funnel. There is a turbine in the narrowest part. The water level inside the chamber rises rapidly and forces air inside, up past the turbine blades. The blades spin a shaft operating a generator. As the wave retreats, the water level in the chamber drops, rapidly creating a low-pressure space. Higher pressure air outside the chamber rushes into the space. On its way into the chamber, the air operates the turbine, but this time from the opposite direction.

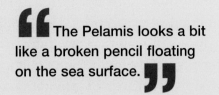

The Pelamis looks a bit like a broken pencil floating on the sea surface.

George Hagerman, US oceanographer and ocean engineer

▽ Each 120-metre-long Pelamis can generate 750 KW of power – the same as many wind turbines in use today.

The pull of the tides

The final source of water power is the rise and fall of ocean tides. Unlike all other forms of water energy, tides are not formed solely by the Sun's energy. They happen because of gravitational attraction, mostly by the Moon but also by the Sun, on the vast mass of water in the oceans. The Moon orbits Earth in a roughly egg-shaped path throughout each day. Therefore, it is closest to Earth twice a day and furthest away twice a day. High tides happen when the Moon is closest and the gravitational pull is greatest. Low tides happen when the Moon is furthest away from Earth.

> **❝ Think about the movement of the waves, the ebb and flow, the to-and-fro motion of the tides, the ocean is a vast amount of lost power. ❞**
>
> Victor Hugo in *Ninety-Three*, 1874

▽ The tidal barrage on the Rance river, France, was opened in 1967. You can see the moving water going through sluice gates and past turbines beneath the part of the barrage nearest the foot of the page.

Tidal range

Tidal range is the difference in height between high and low tides. The largest tidal ranges of the year happen when the Sun and Moon are pulling in the same direction or in exactly opposite directions. The typical tidal range at the coast is between 1.8 and 3 metres. However, some places have much higher tidal ranges owing to the coastal shape and ocean floor profile. The world's greatest tidal range is 17 metres, in the Bay of Fundy, Canada. This is because the bay's circular shape causes water to slosh back and forth every 12 hours – the same amount of time that lapses between high tides.

Harnessing tidal power

People harness tidal energy in two main ways. Tidal barrage installations are rather like low dams across the mouth of an estuary with a large tidal range. The barrage has sluice gates and inbuilt turbines. As a tide comes in, water builds up on the seaward side of the barrage, creating a large head of water relative to the inland side. At high tide, water is released through gates past the turbines. The gates are then closed as the tide goes out and the process is reversed.

Tidal turbines are more like underwater wind turbines attached to the sea bed. Underwater currents develop in coastal waters as tides ebb and flow. They are especially fast where currents flow through narrow channels, or around headlands. As seawater is so dense, the energy in a current moving at 12 kilometres per hour is equivalent to wind moving at over 300 kilometres per hour. Unlike winds, the currents are also relatively predictable as the tide comes in and goes out every 12 hours.

THE ARGUMENT: Tidal power is more reliable than wave power

For:
- High tides happen twice a day every day.
- Tidal power installations do not have to be as robust as wave power systems.

Against:
- Tides vary in height throughout the year, so the head of water at a barrage varies.
- There are few sites worldwide with a large tidal range.
- Waves are more variable than tides but have much more energy.

CHAPTER 3 | Water power in practice

Water power happens at a wide range of scales, providing electricity to single households or whole regions. It presents a variety of installation challenges, from designing dams to building wave-proof machines.

Small-scale installations

Small-scale hydropower, or microhydro, projects are ideal for supplying energy cheaply in remote settlements near small, powerful rivers. These places are often unconnected to the electrical grid. Any river is narrowest and fastest on hills and mountains – the highest points in the catchment area – because gradients and therefore head of water are greatest. Microhydro is commonly used in the Himalayas of Asia, and in mountains in East Africa and Norway. It is used in parts of both more economically developed countries (MEDCs) and less economically developed countries (LEDCs).

Microhydro schemes typically produce less than 100 KW of power per day. This is enough to supply up to 500 average homes in LEDCs, but fewer

▽ These small-scale hydropower facilities, on the Luang Namtha river in Laos, were made using locally available materials.

than 100 average households in MEDCs, which rely more on electrical appliances such as dishwashers, washing machines and computers. Many microhydro schemes are much smaller than this, sometimes supplying power to just a few individuals.

The output of a microhydro system can vary throughout the year, so it is sometimes supplemented by solar power. This works well because there is most solar power when it is sunniest – the time when flow rate often starts to drop in small rivers.

CASE STUDY: Mountain power

Ghandruk is a village in Nepal in the enormous Annapurna mountain range of the Himalayas. Its villagers, like 90 per cent of Nepalese people, have no access to the electrical grid because the country is too poor to develop it – and because the steep slopes around Ghandruk make the challenge of linking it to a grid almost impossible. In 1990, many of the villagers worked together to create a run-of-river micro-hydro power installation on the Modi Khola river. They were given technical assistance by two charities promoting renewable energy.

The villagers dug a 2-kilometre channel from the river to a settling basin. This is a pond where sand and stones in river water sink to prevent them damaging the turbine. They built a powerhouse for the turbine and generator, and dug a penstock between basin and turbine. The head of water is over 200 metres. The Pelton-type turbine, built in Nepal and simple for local people to maintain, is designed to work efficiently no matter how river flow varies throughout the year. Wires from the generator take electricity to 272 households. A moving belt from the shaft is also attached to power a communal rice-milling machine.

In 1992, the generator was up and running. Ghandruk villagers use the power mostly for lighting and cooking. The use of new electric stoves in the village rather than traditional wood-fired stoves is a big improvement. People are conserving local forests by cutting down fewer trees for fuelwood. And children and women spend less time collecting fuelwood and more time learning to read and write, which is easier with electric lights.

Large hydropower plants

The biggest hydropower plants provide a power output in excess of 2,000 MW – enough to supply many settlements and industries. Large projects like this are expensive to build, so they have to be planned very carefully. First, engineers calculate how many turbines and generators are needed to output the power required by the users. Although it costs more to buy and install bigger turbines, it is often relatively less expensive than installing lots of smaller turbines that

△ The Kariba dam is set in a gorge on the Zambezi river between Zambia and Zimbabwe. This aerial view clearly shows its arched shape, which gives the dam extra strength to back up its solid construction.

add up to the same power output. Experts then calculate the reservoir sizes needed to supply the optimum flow rate and head. They use rainfall and river flow rate records to assess how rapidly a reservoir will naturally fill. To cope with peak demands for electricity, hydropower plants are sometimes planned with a secondary reservoir to enable pumped storage (see pages 12–13).

Dam building

In general, increased hydropower output requires bigger reservoirs held in place by bigger dams. A dam is not just a solid wall. It is constructed to withstand water pressure trying to push it outwards. In cross-section, any dam is thickest at its base where pressure is greatest. From above, many dams curve in towards the reservoir. This arched shape is stronger than a straight dam. The strength of a dam also depends on the materials used. Solid concrete or a thin concrete skin over compacted soil or rock may be chosen, depending on the weight of water to hold back. In some regions that are prone to earthquakes, dams also have to have the flexibility to remain strong without shattering when the ground shakes.

There are many challenges during dam construction. For example, concrete releases heat as it sets. When this happens in the enormous amounts of concrete poured to form a giant dam, the heat can produce cracks that weaken the dam walls. Construction workers use water pipes to cool down setting concrete to ensure a dam is strong.

CASE STUDY: Building a megadam

The Itaipu dam, on the Brazil-Paraguay border, is the largest in the world and took around 40,000 people 17 years to build. The main dam is nearly 200 metres high, houses 20 turbines and has penstocks a bus could pass through side-on. Brazil would need to burn 434,000 barrels of oil every day to produce the same power as this dam – 80,000 GWh (gigawatt hours) per year. Before building the dam, workers first had to divert the Parana river (the seventh-largest river in the world) to dry out the riverbed. This took nearly three years. Engineers and workers used heavy machinery and explosives to remove 50 million tonnes of rocks, creating a 2-kilometre-long, 100-metre-deep diversion channel. Once the main dam was complete, the diversion channel was closed off. It took just two weeks for the Parana's waters to fill the 1,350 square-kilometre reservoir.

Developing wave power machines

The French inventor Girard and his son saw the potential of using waves to power machines more than 200 years ago. However, it took until about 1970 for machines to be built that could actually create electricity. Different scientists have produced various designs for wave power machines, many floating and some built into coasts, with names such as Mighty Whale and Pendulor. Once designs work in theory, scientists build working scale models to test in wave tanks in laboratories. The tanks make waves in the range of sizes that the machine might face in real seas, and specialist equipment monitors the power produced.

If a model of a design appears to work, the next step is to make a full-size working prototype. Sometimes this is not possible owing to high costs, or difficulties in making the technology work at a larger scale.

▽ The toughened concrete Limpet wave machine (see page 16) is attached firmly to the rocks to withstand the impact of Atlantic waves.

CASE STUDY:
The cruel sea

In 1995, scientists in Scotland were ready to test the prototype of their promising wave power machine called Osprey. It was a tall, 750-tonne steel structure designed to squat on the sea floor, with its top above the surface, and worked rather like Limpet (see pages 17–18 and picture left). Engineers used floating cranes to position Osprey 100 metres offshore on a warm, calm day in August when waves should have been small. However, a storm blew up, bringing unusually high waves. These cracked open huge empty metal tanks, designed to be filled with sand to anchor Osprey in one spot. Without sand inside they were weak. The cracks were mended, and costly generators and other equipment were saved, but the high waves damaged the tanks further. Eventually, Osprey toppled over and sank.

For example, Salter's Nodding Duck is a wave machine design that worked well as a model but has never been made. This is because its system to convert the rise and fall of waves into spinning a turbine is too complex and expensive to build. Some prototypes have failed simply because they cannot survive real conditions in the oceans.

Destructive forces

The ocean is a challenging place to install floating and fixed wave power machines. The strength of waves can damage materials as tough as steel, push machines around or even topple them over. Waves become stronger with increasing depth of water, but anchoring machines to the sea floor becomes more difficult and expensive with depth, because it requires the expertise of specialist divers. Unlike a river, there is no way to hold back the sea while installing a wave machine. Oceans 50–100 metres deep offer the right balance between wave energy and ease of installing wave machines.

It was not the best day I've had, but we learned a lot from it.

Allan Thomson, head of the UK company that built Osprey, after it was destroyed

CHAPTER 4
Living with water power

Water power affects landscapes, communities and the planet. Not surprisingly, people's opinions are strongly divided about the pros and cons of this renewable energy source.

Changing the landscape

The largest reservoirs and dams on Earth are so big that they can be seen from space. Enormous hydropower plants change the look of land dramatically – for example, whole valleys are flooded and roads are built around dam sites to transport workers and building materials. But even small hydropower systems have an impact.

Silt washed off land by stream and river water collects at the bottom of reservoirs. This may make river water downstream of a dam clearer, but it also prevents silt from washing onto land. Silt increases the fertility of soil naturally when it floods onto land, helping crops to grow – so a dam may make downstream farmland less productive. Silt trapped behind dams can be dredged or flushed through the sluice gates to keep reservoirs functioning. However, trapped silt reduces global reservoir capacity by up to 1 per cent each year. If reservoirs are getting shallower, some people ask, is hydropower actually renewable?

Building a dam can also transform the land in a very positive way. A main function of dams is controlling river flow in order to prevent downstream flooding. The reduction of soil fertility needs to be balanced against the human and material costs of severe flooding in river settlements.

THE ARGUMENT:
Large hydropower plants do not harm land

For:
- Losing some land is acceptable to create clean power.
- Scientists study earthquake records to assess the danger of any reservoir.
- Measures are usually taken to slow down silt build-up.

Against:
- Areas of land are often flooded to create dams, and rivers are forced to change.
- Reservoirs can cause earthquakes.
- Dams trap river silt, affecting farming and fishing and potentially causing flooding.

Potential problems

Some scientists believe that reservoirs over 100 metres deep, in mountainous areas, can cause earthquakes. Many mountain ranges grow along faults, which are lines where parts of the Earth's crust move against, over or under one another. The weight of water in a reservoir presses on the rock underneath, forcing water in the rocks to move through and open cracks. This weakens the crust and makes it more likely to slip apart. An example of this phenomenon was the 1967 earthquake that killed 200 people soon after the reservoir behind Koyna dam in India was filled.

▽ The vast structure of the Three Gorges dam can be seen from space. Some people believe the dam's reservoir poses a serious flood risk.

CASE STUDY: Damming the Yangtze

The Three Gorges dam on the Yangtze river, China, will be able to generate one-and-a-half times the power of Itaipu (see page 23) when it starts operation in 2009. This should provide power for millions of people, greatly reducing the country's use of fossil fuels. But will the dam create problems? The Yangtze carries a lot of silt from its dusty catchment area. Critics say this silt will build up quickly in the reservoir behind the dam, raising the reservoir floor and risking flooding over the top of the dam. This would be ironic because the dam's other main purpose is to prevent downstream flooding that has killed millions of people. The Chinese government plans to dam other rivers in the area and use newly designed silt traps to lessen the problems, but their effectiveness remains to be seen.

Dams and displaced people

Worldwide, some 40–80 million people have been displaced by 48,000 dam projects, many built to supply hydropower. When settlements are flooded, people have to find new places to live and work – sometimes in different regions or even countries.

△ These people in India are protesting against a series of more than 3,000 planned dams on the Narmada river that will displace millions.

The biggest hydropower projects can cause mass migration of people and put great pressure on resources, such as drinking water or food, in the places they move to. As outsiders, migrants may be unfamiliar with the local language or culture, and the poorest, least powerful may end up living in much worse conditions than before. For example, they may end up farming on less fertile farmland or living in more cramped housing.

> ❝The direct adverse impacts of dams have fallen disproportionately on rural dwellers, subsistence farmers, indigenous peoples, ethnic minorities, and women.❞
>
> Final Report Fact Sheet, Dams and Development, World Commission on Dams, 2001

Changing lives

In most cases, people are paid to move out of the way of reservoirs and dams, and are compensated for any crops or land they have had to leave behind.

However, sometimes there is not enough money to restore their livelihoods straight away, so they either have to wait long periods to be paid or may not ever get the money they are owed. For example, displaced people waited up to 15 years for compensation after the Aswan dam in Egypt was built.

Most hydropower schemes claim to improve lives, perhaps through supplying power or by providing new industries associated with the reservoir, such as recreation. But many schemes have no such effect. Nam Theun hydropower scheme in Laos, for example, was built to export power to Thailand, so Laotian people have had little benefit from its construction.

Unfair distribution

In some cases, the electricity from big dams does not reach local, rural people whose lives could be greatly improved – even though there is a grid in place. This is because governments prioritize power for cities, businesses and export, for example, to make more money. Half of all Paraguayans have no power even though their country co-owns the world's largest hydropower facility, Itaipu (see page 23). For people who live near reservoirs, the large areas of still waters can even bring illness from disease-carrying insects that breed there.

THE ARGUMENT: Hydropower does not damage people's lives

For:
- Reservoirs are not just for hydropower: they supply clean water to drink, stop devastating natural floods and provide recreation space.

- Displaced people are compensated and may also move to better areas.

- Not all hydropower schemes need people to move – for example run-of-river projects (see page 11).

Against:
- Poor migrants have little choice over where they move to and may end up in worse places than those they came from. Many do not benefit from the hydropower schemes that displace them.

- Migrants may lose not only their way of life and homes, but also ancestral places important to their culture.

- Compensation is often inadequate and may not be paid to people who desperately need it for a long time after they have been displaced.

Pollution problems

Reservoirs in hydropower installations do not supply entirely clean energy because they can cause air pollution. When vegetation is flooded behind dams, it rots in the water and releases greenhouse gases, including methane, from the reservoir surface. Normally pollution that runs off farmland and land near factories is washed by rivers into the oceans, where it may disperse.

◁ Lake Moogerah, in Queensland, Australia, was created by damming a river and flooding rare rainforest habitats. The tops of the dead trees are seen here, poking out of the water.

CASE STUDY: Wildlife rescue

The Kariba hydropower dam (see picture page 22) was built on the Zambezi river in Zimbabwe, in 1958. As its reservoir filled, land animals became stranded on islands. Charities raised money to save the animals. Wildlife rangers in boats rescued some, including snakes and monkeys, using nets. They fired sedative darts at large animals such as rhinos and elephants, then transported them on makeshift rafts to new habitats. In total, 700 animals were saved but many more drowned or starved as their food was submerged.

Reservoirs can store and concentrate pollutants washed off land from entire catchment areas. It is estimated that pollution upstream of China's Three Gorges dam (see page 27) will double, because the facility will trap more than 50 kinds of pollutants. These include untreated human sewage and lead and mercury used in factories and quarries.

Affecting ecosystems

Hydropower reservoirs destroy and change wildlife habitats. Flooding land can kill some animals outright or force them to move elsewhere. In still reservoir water containing concentrated nutrients from river silt, surface plants such as water hyacinth may thrive. These cut out light and oxygen that tiny plants and animals below need to survive. Water released through dams from deep reservoirs is often so cold that certain fish and other wildlife cannot survive in downstream parts of rivers.

Dams block the natural movements of many river animals. For example, salmon normally cannot breed unless they travel upstream to pools where they hatched. Dams prevent this, unless they have fish ladders – a series of stepped sluices – at the side. Wetlands are areas of marshy land where slow-moving rivers spill across land. When dams reduce river flow rate, wetlands can dry up, destroying a vital habitat for wildlife ranging from frogs and insects to fish and birds. Dried-up coastal wetlands cannot provide an effective barrier against seawater flooding. Salty conditions can harm not only farmland but also communities of plants and animals. However, reservoirs can also create habitats – for example they make good stopover sites for migrating birds.

THE ARGUMENT: Hydropower does not damage the environment

For:
- Hydropower causes less atmospheric pollution than non-renewable energy sources.
- River habitats change naturally, not just because of dams, and wildlife can often adapt to new situations.
- Scientists study potential reservoir sites and recommend using places where wildlife, especially rare types, is least affected.

Against:
- Reservoirs concentrate pollution from land and release atmospheric pollution.
- Dams block animal movements.
- Changing water flow in rivers affects and even destroys habitats.

Sharing water

Rivers often cross international borders – over 40 per cent of the world's population lives in a catchment area shared by two or more countries. Many nations have agreements over sharing water fairly, but it is complicated balancing the needs of industry, farmers and growing cities. The Mekong river is one of the longest in Asia, passing through China, Laos, Thailand, Cambodia and Vietnam. These countries have water-sharing agreements, but dams built to provide hydropower on the river in China have reduced water flow in the other countries. This has affected industries such as fishing and rice production.

Some countries remove dams to resolve water-sharing issues. For example, some US states are decommissioning, or removing, some old hydropower dams to restore fishing industries. Small hydropower plants and run-of-river installations have no dams so have little effect on water flow. In some cases, people may actually become better at using shared water resources if they all have a stake in a shared hydropower installation that benefits them.

Hydropower and conflict

Cutting off water supply from the enemy is a centuries-old tactic used in war. Large hydropower schemes are sometimes destroyed in times of

CASE STUDY: Restoring fisheries

For centuries, the Klallam Native American people lived and fished along the Elwha river, Washington state, USA. Two dams were built on the river in the early 20th century for hydropower to run a paper mill. After that, salmon and steelhead trout numbers dropped, as did numbers of fish-eating animals including grizzly bears and bald eagles. The reservoirs flooded important grazing land for deer. The Klallam people had to move away from the area because their sources of food were lost. Now the US Interiors Department wants to reinstate the fishery by decommissioning the dams. This will involve removing not only the dams, but also around 11 million cubic metres of trapped silt. Although the project will be expensive, it should increase fish numbers by eight times. Income from their capture and sale will benefit the displaced Klallam people and the Elwha ecosystem should be restored.

△ Nalubaale Power Station (Owen Falls dam) controls flow of the Nile river near its source at Lake Victoria, Uganda. There is a water-sharing agreement between Uganda and Egypt, which lies downstream of the dam.

conflict by opposing sides to cut off power supply. For example, hydropower plants were destroyed by US planes during the Afghanistan war of 2001. Terrorists could potentially target big hydropower dams in future, to threaten settlements downstream with disastrous flooding. Another level of conflict is conventional warfare over plans to use shared river water. For example, plans by India to dam the Indus river, partly for hydropower, have caused tension and fighting between India and Pakistan, their downstream neighbours.

THE ARGUMENT:
Hydropower does not cause water conflict

For:
- Small hydropower projects create minimal water-sharing difficulties.

- There are many positive water-sharing agreements between countries worldwide. Some could actually lead to increased availability of water.

Against:
- Large dams and reservoirs can affect downstream communities and industries.

- Hydropower installations may be targeted during conflicts.

Sea changes

Tidal and wave power projects are not used extensively at present. One reason for this is that some people think they are a potential hazard to shipping. They also believe that tidal barrages spoil estuary habitats. Studies of the Rance estuary, France, since a barrage was built in 1967, have noted several changes over time. The barrage has slowed outgoing tides so that there is more silt in the river. But while this has caused a reduction in fish such as plaice, there has been an increase in others such as sea bass. There is no evidence that tidal turbines or wave power machines harm wildlife – the turbines revolve too slowly to injure fish or ocean mammals. In some cases, tidal barrages create surfaces for shells such as mussels to live on, and these provide food for fish and seabirds.

Coastal development

Ocean power plants can bring coastal development in the form of new housing, roads and industry. On the one hand, this changes and may spoil landscapes. On the other, it can bring work and infrastructure to isolated areas. Not all sea power developments take up more land. Houses and other buildings could be built on large tidal barrages, and wave power plants may be worked into existing harbour walls.

THE ARGUMENT: Tidal barrages do not harm estuary habitats

For:
- Barrages change the flow of tides and do not stop them.
- Populations of some species increase after barrages are built.
- Strong currents in areas with high tidal range suitable for tidal power may lack marine life anyway.

Against:
- Barrages may reduce populations of shells and plants living in estuaries and affect animals such as waterbirds that feed on them.
- Barrages block upstream migration of marine animals.

> " Constructing a 10-mile [16-kilometre] concrete energy dinosaur will cause irreversible damage to Wales and England's most important estuaries. "
>
> Morgan Parry, Head of WWF, Cymru, Wales, referring to the proposed Severn barrage.

CASE STUDY:
The Severn barrage

Plans have been submitted to the UK government to build a 16-kilometre long tidal barrage beween England and Wales. This would house more than 200 40-MW turbine/generator systems. Once operational, it could produce the same amount of electricity each year as burning 16 million tonnes of coal in a power station, or from running three nuclear power stations.

Environmental groups are concerned about the the scheme's impact on the Severn estuary. They say that a barrage would reduce tidal range, potentially affecting the Severn river inland. With reduced washing of seawater over mudflats, there would be fewer animals that feed on bits in the water, living in the mud. Then there would be far fewer

△ The Severn estuary is one of the major wetland habitats for birds in Europe.

wading birds. At present the Severn estuary is a home during the year for more than 63,000 geese, ducks and other birds.

However, groups in favour of the barrage say it would bring economic benefit to the region, including clean power for new industries and a road linking the two countries. They say that the Severn estuary is rather like a desert, with little plant and animal life relative to its area, because strong currents churn up a lot of silt in the water. A barrage could calm currents, reducing silt in the estuary and bringing fish to live in the clearer waters.

CHAPTER 5

The economics of water power

How widely water power is used is partly to do with its cost relative to other energy sources and whether it can supply enough energy on demand. But there are other factors encouraging water power, such as government policies.

Supply and demand

Demand for electricity fluctuates throughout the day and year. People use more electricity during the day when they are awake, and most when the weather is very cold or very hot. Electrical companies have to supply electricity to meet these changing demands. Baseload power is the amount they need to produce all the time. Hydropower is a good source of baseload because its energy source, moving water, is cheap and reliable. Precipitation collects in rivers and reservoirs following generally predictable weather patterns. Large hydropower plants have such big reservoirs that they can often supply

▽ Workers in a power station monitor and control power demand and supply, with the help of a bank of gauges and display dials.

baseload even when water levels are down. Pumped storage systems are not generally affected by precipitation, although there is some loss of water from any reservoir through evaporation. Hydropower plants can also react quicker to peak demand than many other power sources – seconds after opening a sluice gate, water reaches the turbines.

Tidal power systems can generate electricity for only about 12 hours a day, and the head of water they operate with varies throughout each month with tidal range. Nevertheless, tides happen predictably every day. Wave power systems cannot operate in calm seas, but they do supply more power from bigger, more powerful waves during cold winters, when electricity is in greater demand.

The price of power
Hydropower requires a substantial initial investment, but after that the operating costs are low. Turbines usually last for a long time – up to 50 years – and require little maintenance. In addition, there are no fuel costs and pollution is low compared with some other power-producing systems.

However, large-scale hydropower involves extra costs compared with microhydro. These include the price of land, dam and reservoir construction, compensation for displaced people and connection to the grid.

Once any hydropower system is in operation, people pay to use the electricity. Hydropower is the cheapest way to generate electricity with present technology. For each kilowatt produced every hour, hydropower costs as little as one twentieth of the price of solar power, a quarter of the price of electricity made in coal power stations and half the price of nuclear power. Ocean power costs about eight times more than hydropower, largely because most systems in use are one-offs at present.

**CASE STUDY:
Water saves trees**

There are around 45,000 microhydro plants in China, many small enough to fit into a village hut. They are generating renewable power for some 300 million people across rural China. In Sichuan province alone, there are 1.5 million people whose only electricity for heating and cooking comes from hydropower. The amount they use has saved the equivalent of 40 million cubic metres of fuelwood each year. That is about the same as a forest of 4 million average-sized oak trees.

Funding water power

Large hydropower and tidal projects are generally so expensive that individuals or single companies cannot pay for them. They are funded partly using loans from private investors, such as multinational banks, and partly by governments or regions. This is because many dams and reservoirs are multipurpose, for example supplying irrigation as well as power. Smaller microhydro projects are often funded partly by individuals, small companies and power co-operatives, which invest money at the outset in return for some payment for electricity sold. Charities and other non-governmental organizations (NGOs), funded largely by donors, may give money for power schemes, helping in development of communities.

Stakeholders

A stakeholder in a planned water power project is any group or individual who can affect or who is affected by the project. This includes power companies, engineers, funding organizations, local people who will live near or be forced to move by the project, and environmental groups trying to conserve endangered wildlife in the area. Part of the money used for any water power scheme is for feasibility studies. People pay experts such as river scientists and ecologists to assess the likely effects of a scheme

on the surrounding area. All stakeholders must assess the pros and cons before a project goes ahead.

> " From the beginning, the Three Gorges dam has been a political project, promoted only by those who would have personal, financial and political gain. "
>
> Dai Qing, journalist, Beijing, China

Incentives

There are many incentives to starting water power schemes, apart from a need for electricity in a particular area. One is obligation. Most countries are signed up to the Kyoto protocol. This is an international agreement, created in 1996 by the United Nations which had previously established the link between greenhouse gases and global warming. The protocol sets out specific targets to cut greenhouse gas emissions by 5 per cent, compared with 1990 levels, before 2012. To achieve this, some governments require power companies to supply part of their electricity by non-polluting means, including water power. Another incentive is international profile. Big projects such as the Three Gorges dam are better showcases for engineering and technological ability than small ones. They prove a country can 'think big' in making development happen fast. However, many small projects may have wider benefits and fewer environmental costs.

CASE STUDY:
Ignoring the experts

A hydropower dam across a gorge on the Turkwell river, Kenya, promised a source of cheap power when it was planned in the 1960s. However, scientists advised against it because the gorge lies on a fault line with a history of earthquakes, and the river flow is far too variable. Experts warned that the reservoir might not fill sufficiently and the reduced water downstream would badly affect forest habitats where local Turkana people lived.

Nevertheless, in 1993 the dam was built, costing three times more than was planned. It is alleged that certain Kenyan politicians gave the go-ahead partly because they were bribed. As predicted, the dam has failed. It produces only half the power it is supposed to, and many types of plants and animals in the downstream habitat are now at risk.

▷ The water level in the Turkwell Gorge hydroelectric dam is too low to produce much power in this arid part of Kenya.

CHAPTER 6 | Water power present and future

Water power is a significant part of the world energy mix now – and in the future it could increase in importance, with more widespread use and changes in water power technology. The future of Earth's energy will also require people to use power more efficiently.

Hydropower today

In 2006, about one-fifth of all electricity generated worldwide was made using water energy, mostly hydropower. Some countries, such as Norway, Nepal and Ethiopia get over 90 per cent of their power from this renewable resource. However, there is great variation in the amount of power produced. For example, whereas 300,000 GW per year of hydropower is generated in both the USA and

▽ This world map shows the percentage of water power out of the total electricity generated by different countries around the world in 2000.

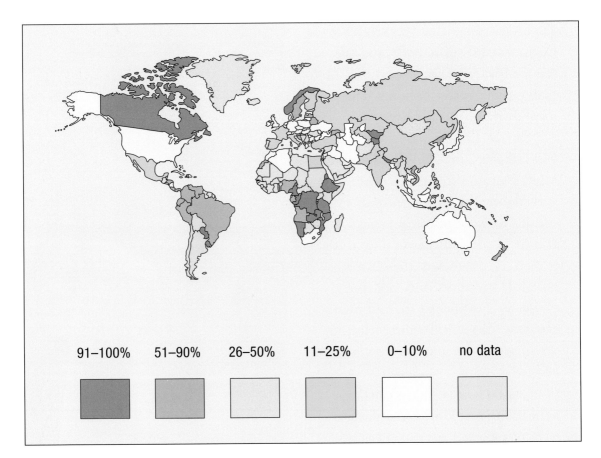

| 91–100% | 51–90% | 26–50% | 11–25% | 0–10% | no data |

Brazil, this is 90 per cent of the Brazilian total but just 7 per cent of the US total of electricity generated. This is because Brazilians on average use far less power than US citizens. Which country or region uses water power depends on both geography and political will. Canada, for example, produces the most hydropower in the world, partly because its government promotes this type of energy.

The future of hydropower

In theory, given water resources worldwide, there could be twice or even three times as much hydropower in future. The greatest potential is in Africa and Asia, and there are many giant dam projects already planned in LEDCs such as the Democratic Republic of Congo.

However, not all of these projects will actually happen because they are very expensive and more people doubt that the benefits outweigh the human and environmental costs. Many people foresee the increased use of cheaper, small-scale hydropower facilities with more efficient low-head turbines. Only 3 per cent of the USA's dams are used for hydropower at present, so in future many of these could be adapted to include turbines and generators. Neither of these scenarios would require the costs of constructing new dams and reservoirs.

The rise of sea power

Power from the sea at present supplies a fraction of 1 per cent of the world's electricity. There are only four commercial-scale tidal barrages and about 12 prototype wave power devices in operation. However, there are around 40 sites identified worldwide for large-scale tidal power. Planned projects include surrounding New York with barrages. The highest wave energy is recorded in seas off north-west Scotland, northern Canada, the north-west and north-east US coasts, southern Africa and Australia. Using existing technology and this potential, some experts believe that wave energy could in future supply 16 per cent of the world's power – not far off what river-based hydropower currently provides.

> **You have to remember that we're at the birth of this technology. What we have achieved now is equivalent to Bleriot [first man to fly across the English Channel] in the early days of aviation.**
>
> Professor Stephen Salter, UK Wave Energy pioneer

New technology

New technology may help people to generate water power in different ways. For example, one idea is to put microturbines in the fresh water flowing through household pipes. This could combine water and electricity supply from one source for remote, off-grid locations. The Hydro Venturi system uses the slight water pressure drop found in narrowing pipes to suck air through turbines. This could harness tides, currents and other moving water energy sources.

Most new wave power designs convert the rise and fall of water into air movement that operates turbines. A US company called Ocean Power Technologies has developed PowerBuoys. These buoys float just beneath the ocean surface and are anchored to the sea floor. They capture

▽ The PowerBuoy generates power from waves and transmits it to land through underwater cables.

and convert wave energy into a mechanical force, driving a generator with no turbine. Sensors ensure the mechanical force is constant in varying wave conditions, and even switch off the generator when waves are too powerful. This protects the equipment from damage. The same company is also developing streamers from buoys that generate electricity when they flex in the moving water.

Responding to the global energy crisis

There are various solutions to the problem of providing power for Earth's growing population. People can mine and extract more non-renewable fuels and adopt better technology to use them more sparingly and in a cleaner way. For example, using carbon filters on power station chimneys prevents greenhouse gases and other pollution from reaching the atmosphere. Scientists can develop new, clean power systems such as hydrogen fuel cells. Nations can also expand their use of renewable energy sources. However, it is equally important to use power resources more carefully. Switching off televisions and computers, rather than leaving them on standby, and fitting electricity-saving lightbulbs, for example, are small power-saving measures – but if everyone does them, less electricity is used.

CASE STUDY: Solving Brazil's power shortage

Brazil is struggling to generate enough power because its existing hydropower dams are too empty after several years with below-average rainfall. The Brazilian government believes the solution is first to ration power but ultimately to build more giant hydropower plants and natural gas power stations. A Brazilian charity called Movement of Dam-Affected People (MAB) has other ideas:

1. Reduce power losses and modernize dam generating equipment, such as turbines: saving 14 GW per year.

2. Construct small hydropower schemes nearer to where people need the power, saving 10 GW per year.

3. Use energy from burning renewable biomass, such as sugar cane waste: saving 3 GW per year.

This total annual saving of more than 27 GW is the same as 40 per cent of the electricity from all Brazil's currently installed hydropower plants. It also has far lower social, environmental and economic costs.

Tomorrow's renewables

Renewable energy sources will provide more of our power in the future. They offer benefits over non-renewable energy sources including reduced pollution and virtually free, plentiful fuel. However, like any power-producing systems, renewables bring social and environmental costs. For water power, the effects of dam building on people and environments are serious concerns.

If all the potential energy in ocean, river and reservoir systems were harnessed, water power could quadruple in future. It is likely that the biggest growth will be in wave and tidal power and microhydro installations. However, different governments will promote different types of renewables in future, so it remains to be seen how significant water power will be in the overall mix.

Power demand

The present rise in energy demand, caused by increasing world population and changing standards of living, is much faster than any non-renewables or renewables can currently provide. Experts predict needs will rise by 50 per cent over the next 20 years, mostly in LEDCs. That is why every individual must make great efforts to reduce power use. It is vital that people develop power-saving habits and use energy-efficient machines to consume less electricity. It is equally vital that governments encourage scientists and engineers to develop new power-production systems, such as hydrogen fuel cells and more efficient turbines, that make more power from the resources we do have while also protecting the planet.

THE ARGUMENT: Moving water will power the future

For:
- Water power is reliable, clean and inexpensive once set up.
- Area for area, water power produces more power than wind farms and solar arrays.
- The potential for expanding tidal and wave power is great; over 90 per cent of our planet is covered with moving seawater!

Against:
- Problems may outweigh the benefits of large hydropower dams.
- The world's demand for power is so great that water can only ever be part of a mix of energy sources.
- Energy saving and new sources of energy are important in finding a solution to the energy crisis.

Climate change

Climate change is one of the greatest challenges facing Earth. In some parts of the world unusually hot, dry weather is causing more widespread forest fires and drought each year. In other parts, unusually stormy, wet weather is causing more floods and landslides. Climate change will affect many renewable energy sources. As Earth becomes warmer, there may be more potential for solar power – but increased heat will cause increased evaporation of reservoirs, reducing hydropower. Increasing rainfall in some catchment areas may cause reservoirs to overflow, with potentially devastating consequences. However, it could also increase flow rate for use in some run-of-river installations. Changing wind patterns will not only affect the positioning of wind farms, but will also impact wave energy.

> **The dinosaurs dominated the Earth for 160 million years. We are in danger of putting our future at risk after a mere quarter of a million years.**
>
> Michael Meacher, UK Minister for the Environment, on global warming in *The Guardian*, 14 February 2003

▽ People watch as a new Pelamis wave machine is installed. Will we see more and more wave power machines off our coasts in the future?

Glossary

Atmosphere Layers of gases that surround Earth.

Baseload The minimum average electricity demand from a power-generating facility.

Catchment area The area of land from which water runs off into a river system.

Estuary The wide, lower part of a river where it nears or meets the sea.

Flow rate The volume of water passing a certain point in a fixed time.

Fossil fuel Natural fuel such as oil, gas or coal, which formed from the remains of living things trapped in layers of rock millions of years ago.

Generator A machine that transforms rotational energy into electrical energy.

Global warming The general, gradual rise in average temperature around the world, caused by greenhouse gases.

Gradient A measure of slope.

Greenhouse gas An atmospheric gas that traps the Sun's heat reflecting off Earth, raising temperatures.

Grid The network of power lines.

Head of water The height of water above turbines in a hydropower unit.

Hydrogen cell A recharging battery that generates electricity through the reaction of hydrogen with oxygen.

Hydropower Electricity generated when falling freshwater turns turbines.

Non-renewable An energy source that is in limited supply and will run out one day, such as coal, oil or gas.

Nuclear power Electricity made by heating water using energy from within atoms (microscopic particles).

Penstock A pipe leading from a reservoir to a turbine.

Precipitation Water that falls during the water cycle, such as rain and snow.

Prototype A working model made and tested as a trial for a real system.

Pumped storage A system where fallen water is pumped back up from a lower reservoir to a higher one to increase its potential energy.

Renewable An energy source that is in limitless supply, such as wind, moving water or sunlight.

Run-of-river A hydropower system installed in the natural course of a river, with no reservoir.

Settling basin A pond for settling silt before river water enters a penstock.

Tidal barrage An installation that traps a head of tidal water to operate a turbine for generating power.

Tidal range The difference in height between low and high tide.

Transformer A machine used to increase or decrease voltage.

Books to read

Energy Essentials: Renewable Energy Nigel Saunders and Steven Chapman, Raintree, 2005: introduces the energy crisis and its many possible solutions.

Going with the Flow Billy Langley and Dan Curtis, Centre for Alternative Technology, 2004: a practical guide to setting up a water power system.

Looking At Energy: Water Power Polly Goodman, Hodder Wayland, 2005: looks at ways people use water to generate electricity.

Water Power (Science Matters) Christine Webster, Weigl Publishers, 2005 and *Hydroelectric Power (Fact Finders: Energy at Work)* Josepha Sherman, Capstone Press, 2004: two good general introductions to water power.

Websites

http://microhydropower.net/index.php   All about microhydro, with a useful pull-down menu featuring detailed information about theory of hydropower and several useful case studies.

http://www.greenpeace.org/international/campaigns/climate-change/solutions/hydroelectric   This website not only has statistics about water power but also gives ways on how you can help to promote the use of microhydro worldwide.

www.practicalaction.org   Provides links to websites of the companies that have developed Pelamis, Limpet and other wave machines.

www.foe.co.uk/resource/briefing/severn_barrage_lagoons.pdf
This site has an interesting discussion about the proposed Severn tidal barrage, its possible effects and benefits and the pros and cons of using tidal lagoons instead.

Note: Page numbers in *italic* refer to illustrations.

ENERGY DEBATE

Contents of all titles in the series:

Nuclear Power 978 07502 5018 4

1. Nuclear power and the energy debate
2. How is energy generated from the atom?
3. Putting nuclear power to work
4. Nuclear Power and the environment
5. Counting the cost of nuclear power
6. Looking ahead to a nuclear-powered future

Wind Power 978 07502 5023 8

1. Wind power and the energy debate
2. How does wind power work?
3. Wind power in practice
4. Living with wind power
5. The economics of wind power
6. Wind power now and in the future

Solar Power 978 07502 5019 1

1. Solar power and the energy debate
2. What is solar power?
3. Harnessing solar power
4. The environment and resources
5. Cost and investment
6. Solar power in the future

Water Power 978 07502 5021 4

1. Water power and the energy debate
2. How water power works
3. Water power in practice
4. Living with water power
5. The economics of water power
6. Water power present and future

Biomass Power 978 07502 5020 7

1. Biomass power and the energy debate
2. What is biomass energy?
3. Biomass in practice
4. The environment and resources
5. Cost and investment
6. Biomass power in the future

Coal, Gas and Oil 978 07502 5022 1

1. Coal, gas and oil and the energy debate
2. What are fossil fuels?
3. Harnessing energy from fossil fuels
4. The environment and resources
5. Cost and investment
6. A fossil fuel-powered future?

WAYLAND